Art In History

Tudor Art

Susie Hodge

Heinemann
LIBRARY

www.heinemann.co.uk/library
Visit our website to find out more information about Heinemann Library books.

To order:
☎ Phone 44 (0) 1865 888112
📄 Send a fax to 44 (0) 1865 314091
🖥 Visit the Heinemann bookshop at www.heinemann.co.uk/library to browse our catalogue and order online.

First published in Great Britain by Heinemann Library, Halley Court, Jordan Hill, Oxford OX2 8EJ, part of Harcourt Education.

Heinemann is a registered trademark of Harcourt Education Ltd.

Editorial: Clare Lewis
Design: Victoria Bevan, Michelle Lisseter, and Q2A Media
Illustrations: Oxford Illustrators
Picture Research: Erica Newbery
Production: Helen McCreath

Printed and bound in Hong Kong by WKT

10 digit ISBN 0 431 05675 7
13 digit ISBN 978 0 431 05675 3

10 09 08 07 06
10 9 8 7 6 5 4 3 2 1

British Library Cataloguing in Publication Data
Hodge, Susie
Art in History: Tudor Art – 2nd edition
709.4'1'09031
A full catalogue record for this book is available from the British Library.

Acknowledgements
The publishers would like to thank the following for permission to reproduce photographs:
A F Kersting p.**26**; A K G Photo p.**14**; Ancient Art & Architecture Collection p.**8**; Bridgeman Art Library: Courtesy of The British Library, London p.**13**, Thyssen – Bornemisza Collection p.**15**, Vatican Museums & Galleries, Rome pp.**10–11**, Victoria & Albert Museum p.**17**; Philip Craven Photo Library p.**25**; Fotomas Index p.**7**; Angelo Hornak Library, courtesy of the Dean & Chapter Westminster Abbey p.**21**; Mansell Collection pp.**9, 12**; National Museum & Gallery, Cardiff p.**4**; National Portrait Gallery, London pp.**16, 19, 28**; National Trust Photographic Library pp.**20, 22, 23, 27**; The Royal Collection © Her Majesty the Queen p.**18**; Thetford Museum p.**29**; Westminster Cathedral Library p**6**.

Cover picture of King Henry VIII by Hans Holbein, reproduced with permission of The Art Archive.

Every effort has been made to contact copyright holders of any material reproduced in this book. Any omissions will be rectified in subsequent printings if notice is given to the publishers.

The paper used to print this book comes from sustainable resources.

Contents

Some words are shown in bold, **like this**.
You can find out what they mean by looking in the glossary.

WHAT IS TUDOR ART?

The Tudor family ruled Britain from 1485–1603. The art of that time shows us what life was like, how ideas developed, and how art changed the way some people thought. Most of all, it shows us what people at that time thought of themselves.

Who paid Tudor artists?

Tudor artists needed to sell their work to earn money. They relied on rich people, especially the royal family, for patronage (payment for work). This might explain why the portraits of royalty were more flattering than written descriptions! Also, artists often had to rely on the patronage of the Church for more work.

Who were the Tudors?

Henry Tudor ruled as King Henry VII from 1485 to 1509. When he died, his son became Henry VIII (from 1509 to 1547). When Henry VIII died, his son, Edward VI, ruled (from 1547 to 1553). The crown went to Edward VI instead of one of his older sisters because the crown always passed to males first. Edward VI was only 16 when he died, and his half-sister succeeded him.

Paintings showing several monarchs were called dynastic paintings. This painting is also an **allegory**. It was painted soon after Elizabeth I became queen. Elizabeth I is on the right, followed by ancient Roman goddesses who symbolized peace and wealth. Edward VI is between Elizabeth I and Henry VIII. On the left are Mary I and her husband, Philip of Spain, followed by Mars, the god of war. Elizabeth I wanted to tell people that she would bring peace and prosperity to the country, while her sister Mary I had brought only trouble.

The Tudor Succession, c. 1570, Lucas de Heere (1534–84), 131 x 18cm (171 x 72 in), oil on panel

The Tudor Rose

The Tudor Rose was designed for Henry VII when he married Elizabeth of York. This marriage ended the wars between the Lancastrians and Yorkists. His rose united the white rose of York with the red rose of Lancaster.

She was Mary I (queen from 1553 to 1558). Henry VIII's other daughter, Elizabeth I (queen from 1558 to 1603), **succeeded** Mary I as the last of the Tudors. She never married and did not have any children. When she died, the crown passed to her cousin James Stuart, which ended the Tudor age.

ART AND RELIGION

In 1485 England was a Catholic country. So were most other countries in Europe. The head of the Catholic Church was the Pope. The Pope was very powerful – he ruled his own country as well as being the head of the Catholic Church everywhere.

Mary I "touching the scrofula", 1556, book illustration

Tudor people believed that their king or queen was chosen by God and so had special powers. Here, Mary I touches a sick person in order to heal her.

Pictures and prayers

Church services were in Latin which most people did not understand. So church walls were painted with scenes from the Bible and other holy images that could be understood. Rich people sometimes bought paintings, statuettes, or ornaments for the Church. They believed that this would please God and mean they would go to heaven when they died.

Religious changes

Some people began to complain about the Catholic Church. They said that it was too rich and powerful and that services should be in the people's own language. The protesters began new Christian churches, called Protestant churches. In Tudor England many arguments followed between Protestants and Catholics.

Kings, queens, and religious problems

When Henry VIII wanted to divorce his first wife, Catherine, and marry his second wife, Anne, the Pope would not allow it. So Henry went against the Pope and made himself the Head of the Church in England. Edward VI believed in Protestant ideas, but he was succeeded by Mary I who was a Catholic. Elizabeth I was a Protestant but she was understanding about other religions.

How art was affected

Catholics and Protestants believed that the way they worshipped God would make a difference as to whether they went to heaven or hell when they died. People from both churches were prepared to die for their beliefs. Wars were fought and art was affected. Protestants preferred not to have wall paintings, expensive statues, or ornaments.

Bishop's Bible, 1572, Franciscus Hogenburg (1540–90), 28 x 19cm (11 x 7in), frontispiece

This is a page from an English Bible that was printed during Elizabeth I's reign (Elizabeth was a Protestant).

MATERIALS AND METHODS

Tudor artists were among the lowest paid workers. They belonged to **guilds** which had strict rules about prices and ways of working. Guild members who broke the rules were fined. Artists could only set themselves up in business if they were members. Boys who wanted to be artists had to become **apprentices** first and learn in the workshop of a master artist or craftsman.

After seven years, each apprentice produced a "masterpiece" to show that he had done well. Then, if he could pay the large fee needed to become a master in the guild, he could set up a business on his own. If he was too poor he had to become a journeyman. Journeymen were hired and paid by the day.

Artist at work, 1568, Jost Amman (1539–91), 70 x 9cm (28 x 36in), woodcut

This shows an artist painting at an **easel**. His apprentice is busy in the background.

Book printing, 1568, Jost Amman (1539–91), 70 x 90cm (28 x 36in), woodcut

This shows a printer's workshop. The men at the back set each word, letter by letter, into a wooden frame which is the size of a page. At the front, one man puts ink on to the type; the other puts the paper in place.

Ideas and inventions

At the start of Tudor times, ink made from nut juice was being used in Europe. **Pastels** were being used during the period of Elizabeth I's reign. The first pencil was made in 1565 in Switzerland (charcoal had been used before).

Oil paints were also becoming popular. Before, paint had been made by adding egg or wax to dry **pigments** to make a paste. Then a Flemish artist, Jan van Eyck, began mixing walnut or linseed oil with his pigments instead.

The new oil paint dried slowly, so artists could correct their work more easily. Paintbrushes were made by tying hairs around a stick with waxed thread. Artists began to use **canvas** to paint on instead of wood. Canvas was light and could be rolled up to carry easily.

With the invention of the printing press came an increase in the number of books. This meant that new ideas reached people more easily. It also meant that more artists were needed to produce illustrations.

THE REBIRTH OF ART

Tudor art was slowly changed by events taking place in the rest of Europe, especially in Italy and Flanders (Flanders is now part of Belgium and France). People were taking a new interest in the art, **architecture**, science, and literature of ancient Greek and Roman times. Artists also studied mathematics and the human body to make their work look realistic and three-dimensional. This period of time was named the **Renaissance**, which means "rebirth". It continued for nearly 200 years.

A brilliant man

Leonardo da Vinci (1452–1519) was a Renaissance artist, scientist, and engineer. He designed flying machines and submarines long before they were invented. He carefully studied how things were constructed and made thousands of drawings and plans. He wrote down his discoveries in secret "back-to-front" writing.

The School of Athens, c. 1510–12, Raphael (1483–1520), width at its base 7.7m (25ft), **fresco**

Raphael admired both Leonardo and Michelangelo. His brilliantly coloured fresco (one of several he painted for the Pope) represents the great thinkers of ancient Greece. Raphael studied real people including himself and his friends in the painting. The life sized, solid-looking figures are arranged in a perfectly balanced **composition**. Raphael has also used new **perspective** techniques to show space and distance.

The Sistine Chapel ceiling in Rome, 1508–12, Michelangelo (1475–1564), fresco

Michelangelo took four years to paint the whole ceiling. While painting the ceiling he lay flat on his back on wooden scaffolding, 20 metres (65 feet) above the ground. The result of his work is fantastic. The 300 figures in the painting seem to spring out of the ceiling, bringing the Bible to life. It is one of the world's greatest masterpieces.

Michelangelo

Michelangelo Buonarroti was another artist who worked on many different forms of art. He was a painter, sculptor, architect, and poet. He is particularly famous for his sculpture and for his fresco on the ceiling of the Sistine Chapel in Rome.

Lifelike pictures

Renaissance art was full of lifelike details. It was very different to the art completed before the Renaissance, which had become much less realistic. The ideas of the Renaissance were passed on through books and by travellers. But travel was slow and difficult, so it took a long time for the ideas to spread.

ART AND BOOKS

The invention of **movable type** in 1447 made printing books even easier. Books helped to spread new ideas and knowledge. Most early printed books were religious.

Printing pictures

Book illustrations were made by the ancient method of woodcut. First a back-to-front picture was cut into a block of wood and then covered with ink, made of oil and soot. When paper was pressed on to the block, a print appeared the right way round. Some prints were very detailed and tiny tools were needed to cut them. Woodcuts were cheap, easy to produce, and thousands of copies of a picture could be printed from one block.

This is a woodcut from a famous book, showing Protestant **martyrs** being burned for refusing to become Catholics. Some of the book's pictures are quite gruesome. Cranmer was the Archbishop of Canterbury. Catholics burnt him at the stake because he was a Protestant. You can see him stretching his hand into the flame, saying "Lord receive my Spirite". Tudor spelling was different to ours – Frier John was a monk, not a cook!

The Burnyng of Cranmer, from Foxe's Book of Martyrs, 1563, 33 x 18.5cm (13 x 7in), woodcut

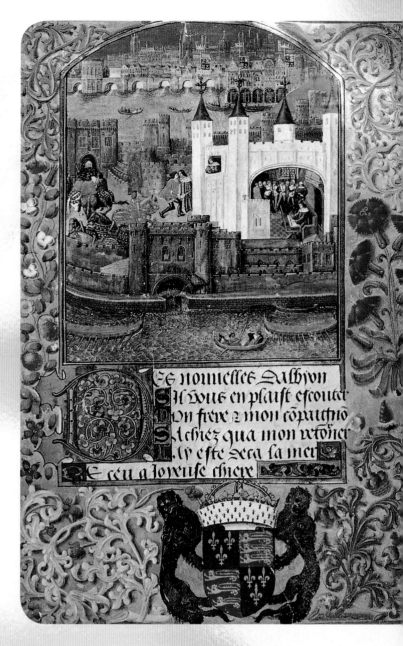

The earliest painting of London, c. 1500, artist unknown

This was for the front of a book of poems by Charles, the Duke of Orleans in France. The **illuminated** letter "D" is an example of how books were illustrated before printing had been invented.

The painting shows the Duke when he was imprisoned in the Tower of London. He is shown at the window of the White Tower, riding through an arch in the tower on the left, and also writing a letter at a desk. The Duke was released in 1440, but we know the picture was painted about 60 years later because the London buildings are painted as they looked in 1500.

Flat pictures

Many of the artists who made woodcuts did not know about the ideas of the Renaissance artists and the use of perspective. Their pictures seem much flatter. Many of the woodcut artists were not as skilled as Renaissance artists.

Painted books

Coloured pictures like this painting of London could not be printed like they can today. Each one had to be painted by hand, so few Tudor books contained coloured pictures.

TUDOR PORTRAITS

Henry VIII was broad-shouldered, with red hair, a long nose, and a small mouth. How do we know this? Because we have **portraits** of the king. The most well-known paintings from Tudor times were portraits commissioned (ordered) by the rich and powerful.

No smiling

The nobility ordered portraits to show their power. Good portrait painters showed people in dark colours with serious expressions, in family groups or alone. One of the most famous portrait painters of Tudor times was Hans Holbein.

*Henry VIII, 1536, Hans Holbein (1497–1543), 28 x 19cm, (11 x 7in) oil and **tempera** on oak*

The black background symbolizes power. The king is looking at the viewer and almost fills the frame. He seems greater than us. His eyes and mouth are stern; his clothes and magnificent jewellery look expensive. This powerful but small portrait was painted in the year that Henry's first wife died, his second wife was beheaded, and he married his third!

Hans Holbein the Younger (1497–1543)

German-born Hans Holbein was the son of a painter. He trained in his father's studio and later moved to Switzerland. There he designed woodcuts. He painted portraits and religious subjects. In 1532 he moved to England and soon found work painting portraits of rich merchants and courtiers. Henry VIII asked Holbein to paint members of the royal household and his fame spread. Holbein died of the plague in London in 1543.

Holbein captured every sitter's personality. People were amazed at how lifelike his subjects looked. Many other artists tried to copy Holbein, but he is still one of the greatest portrait painters in history.

Georg Gisze of Dansig, *1532,*
Hans Holbein (1497–1543), 96
x 86cm (38 x 34in), oil on wood

Holbein painted this when he first arrived in London. Georg was a merchant. You can see his belongings all around him, including his scales and weights and the wax seals for marking documents. Unlike most English artists, Holbein had seen Italian Renaissance paintings and had learned about composition, balance, and how to observe everything closely. See how Georg's eyes look straight at you even though his body is slightly turned away.

A GREAT QUEEN

Elizabeth I lived from 1533 to 1603. During her life many portraits were painted of her, but some did not show what she really looked like. There are many reasons for this. For example, she did not like the idea of growing old and wanted to appear young, even later in life.

Also, she wanted her portraits to influence how people felt about her. She had control over her portrait painters. She sent her favourite artists on tours to far away parts of the country. This meant the artists could not see what she really looked like.

Elizabeth I *(The "Ditchley" Portrait), 1592, Marcus Geeraerts the Younger (1561–1636), 241 x 152cm (95 x 60in), oil on canvas*

This full-length portrait has Elizabeth standing astride the world. Her feet are on England, by Ditchley, where an entertainment had been given in her honour. The Sun represents her glory and the thunder her power.

The picture is detailed but flat-looking. For once the Queen has not been made to look young. As a forceful figure towering over her country, she has been made to look wise and great. She is wearing magnificent clothes and jewels to show her wealth and power.

Miniatures

Miniatures were tiny portraits that became particularly popular during Tudor times. Nicholas Hilliard (1547–1619) was the son of a goldsmith who became chief portrait painter to the queen in 1584. He also painted beautiful miniatures in the tradition of monks' illuminated manuscripts.

How Hilliard made miniatures

First he would cut a playing card into an oval shape and cover it with **vellum**. Next he would coat the vellum with flesh-coloured paint.

He would draw the picture lightly with a pencil and then build up the details gradually, with thin layers of paint and real gold leaf. Hilliard always used clear, brilliant colours, grinding them himself on a crystal block and mixing them with distilled water and **gum arabic**.

You could try making your own miniature with card and paints.

Elizabeth I, *1572, Nicholas Hilliard (1547–1619), 5 x 4.5cm (2 x 1¾in) oil on vellum*

Hilliard always painted Elizabeth I in a clear light with no shadows. His miniatures looked like jewels and were often worn as such.

Actual size

STORYTELLING PICTURES

The Field of the Cloth of Gold, *1520, artist unknown, 168 x 347cm (66 x 135in), oil on panel*

At the beginning of the Tudor period, only Royal or noble homes had paintings. Most of these were portraits of people in the family. By the end of the Tudor period, artists were painting family portraits for more people. They were also painting many other things, from decorations for **pageants** and **masques**, to wooden panelling in houses. Occasionally artists were asked to paint a picture that told a story.

Art for the rich

Only the rich could afford paintings, so poor people were rarely shown in them.

This told the story of Henry VIII's meeting with French king, Francis I, in 1520 in France. The meeting became known as the "Field of the Cloth of Gold" because so much gold cloth was used in the tents and decorations.

The painting features Henry VIII several times. In the front he rides with his attendants with a dragon firework flying above. Towards the back both kings and their queens are watching the jousting from beside a tent.

Sir Henry Unton, *1596, artist unknown, 163 x 74cm (64 x 29in), oil on panel*

Sir Henry Unton was a well-to-do gentleman, landowner, soldier, MP, and the queen's ambassador to France during Elizabeth I's reign. At his widow's request, his life was recorded in this large painting. Find him in his study and at a musical banquet with his wife. Other scenes show his mother; Unton studying at Oxford; travelling in Venice, the Low Countries, and France; on his sick-bed; his body being carried back to England; the funeral procession. Outside his house poor people are mourning his death. This type of storytelling painting was unusual. Maps were more likely to be hung on walls than pictures, and portraits were the most popular paintings.

Paint palette

Tudor artists made paint from grinding natural materials. Charcoal produced black; earth gave browns; chalk produced white. The lapis lazuli stone gave bright blue; copper produced green; a red rock, red; lead-tin, yellow. Sometimes real gold was used, too.

STYLES IN SCULPTURE

Wealthy people paid artists to make paintings of themselves and their families to show how important they were. They also paid sculptors to carve grand tombs for when they died. Tomb sculpture changed during the period just as portrait painting did. It took on the more realistic style of the Renaissance.

Slow changes

By the 1500s, sculptors had begun to copy decorative details from Renaissance artists, but they missed the basic idea of making the human form realistic. Although the tombs were detailed, the figures in them looked stiff and unnatural. Henry VIII employed an Italian sculptor, who had trained with Michelangelo, to create his parents' tomb.

Tomb of William Sharington

William Sharington died in 1553. The sculptor of his tomb carved detailed and precise decorations, making sure that each side matched the other. The tomb is made of **marble**, **alabaster**, and expensive imported materials. Notice the little figures, the crests, and the fancy decorations. This skilful work was in demand. Even the dead had to look fashionable!

The Renaissance reaches Britain

Henry VII's tomb stands out not just because Torrigiano was a great artist, but because of how he worked. The statues' positions, their faces, and clothes are more lifelike and natural-looking than any other sculpture being produced in Britain at the time.

Other work for sculptors

Sculptors were not encouraged to create masterpieces like the Renaissance artists. Although Henry VIII paid for this tomb he did not seem to have been interested in sculpture as decorative art. What the king wanted (or did not want) set the fashion, so few other people wanted decorative sculpture either.

Tombs were almost the only way sculptors could earn money and the **patrons** wanted them to look impressive, not realistic.

Henry VII's tomb in Westminster Abbey, 1512–18, Pietro Torrigiano (1472–1528), **gilt, bronze,** *black and white marble*

Torrigiano came to England from 1511 to 1522. He worked on the two life-size statues of Henry VII and his wife, Elizabeth of York, for four years.

DECORATIVE CARVINGS

Masons, woodcarvers, and stonecarvers decorated buildings, inside and out, with imaginative carvings. The work was valued by how well the materials were used. There were strict guild rules about the materials that should be used. Artists usually worked on the spot, which sometimes meant being high on a roof or beside a window. They carved the fine details by hand using metal tools such as **chisels** and **files**. They signed their work by carving marks or faces into the wood or stone.

Chimney piece from Canons Ashby, Northamptonshire, originally made in about 1590, plaster, brick, and iron

Fires were the only form of heating in Tudor times. Chimneys replaced simple smoke holes in the roof. This meant large fireplaces became an important part of each room. This impressive-looking fireplace was made out of plaster and painted to look like marble, with gold leaf and other coloured paints. The crests were painted in later (in about 1634) and put on top of original oval-shaped painted panels. The blue tiles were also added much later. Designs such as flowers, animals, fruit, leaves, and scrolls were common features on grand Tudor fireplaces. Small carved figures began to replace the plainer pillars and columns during Elizabeth's reign.

In 1505, a wealthy wool merchant had this house built as a wedding present for his son, Thomas Paycocke. There is a lot of carving on both the inside and outside of the house. This man and the leaves have been carved in wood to match other details around the outside of the house.

Panels and patterns

Wallpaper was rare so panelling was popular in Tudor homes and churches. This helped to make the rooms warmer but made them dark. Small squares of wood or panels were fixed to the walls with a grid of wooden strips in front. Patterns were carved into the panels. Sometimes panels were painted to add colour to the room.

Decorations everywhere

Outside walls were decorated mainly around the windows, doors, chimneys, and **buttresses**, with carved animals, angels, and **gargoyles**. The Tudor Rose, designed for Henry VII, was used a lot, so were **fleur-de-lys**, crinkled ribbons, and vines. Ceilings were decorated with complicated plaster patterns. Even rainwater pipes and door hinges were carved into decorative shapes.

23

TUDOR BUILDINGS

Great improvements were made to houses during Tudor times. Architecture developed as new houses were built. Master masons were the chief builders. They designed the buildings and told the other craftsmen (masons, stonecarvers, woodcarvers, glassmakers, and carpenters) what to do.

As well as houses, more schools, colleges, universities, and places to care for the poor were built all over the country. Master masons used materials that were found locally, but stone, red brick, and terracotta became particularly popular.

Make a model Tudor house

Materials:
- **different sized cardboard boxes**
- **card**
- **scissors**
- **sticky tape**
- **pencil**
- **paper**
- **glue**
- **ruler**
- **paint or felt-tipped pens**

1. Stack your boxes together to make up the shape of a house. Glue or tape them into position and paint them white. Shape the top of the house like a roof.

2. Cut out a door. Draw or paint windows on paper rectangles and stick them on.

3. Using a ruler draw the wooden frame. Paint or colour it dark brown or black. Fold some card for the roof. Paint it reddish-brown to look like terracotta (clay) tiles or a yellow-brown to look like straw thatch. Stick it on the house.

How houses were built

Many well-off people had half-timbered houses. They had a stone or brick base to stop dampness from damaging the walls. A wooden frame was built on top, called wattle, and the gaps in between were filled with daub, which could be made with mud, chopped straw, and manure. Plaster was put over the daub. Instead of holes in the roof to let out smoke, proper brick chimneys were built. This was a great improvement because up until then houses were filled with smoke.

Many of these houses had glass windows of small diamond-shapes, fixed together with lead strips. Glass was expensive. If people could not afford glass, they used pieces of polished horn. Some houses had no upstairs rooms, just high ceilings. Others had upstairs rooms that stuck out, which were called jetties. These made upstairs rooms bigger and protected downstairs rooms from bad weather.

Well-off people left money in their wills for almshouses to be built, to give poor people somewhere to live.

Almshouses, Windsor Castle

CASTLES AND COURTS

The Tudors brought peace to England after many years of fighting. Great homes no longer had to be defended against attack. So people built grand mansions and manor houses which were designed to be comfortable homes and not fortresses.

Styled to impress

Rich Tudors wanted impressive homes, so master masons experimented with new styles. They mixed Italian Renaissance designs with English ideas and made buildings that looked as magnificent as ancient castles but were more comfortable. Stone was the most common building material, but red brick became popular too. Because glass was expensive, large windows became a symbol of wealth, as were tall decorated chimneys. Windows were sometimes filled with **stained glass**. They looked like transparent oil paintings.

Hampton Court Palace, Surrey, building began 1514, master mason Henry Redman (died 1528), red brick

This was first built for Cardinal Wolsey, but he gave it to Henry VIII in 1529. It was made almost entirely of rose-red bricks. Craftsmen from several countries worked on the magnificent building, carving detailed decorations both inside and out.

How stained-glass windows were made

First an artist drew the design on a whitewash-coated table. Then the shapes, sizes, positions, and colours of the pieces of glass were marked on the table. A heated iron tool was used to cut the glass to the right shapes. Any rough edges were smoothed. The pieces of glass were then laid on the table over the design.

The artist painted on any details with special paint. Next, the glass pieces were laid out on an iron plate, covered with ashes, and heated in a **kiln**. This made the paint stick to the glass. After the glass had cooled, lead was moulded round each piece of glass and the picture was put together like a jigsaw.

This stained-glass window shows Catherine of Aragon, Henry VIII's first wife, kneeling. The rich colours are clear, yet the picture is detailed. The textures of the materials and pillars have been painted to look realistic. Notice the little dog curled up asleep and the gentle landscape in the background. Stained-glass windows were a great luxury in Tudor times.

Stained-glass window, from the chapel at The Vyne, Northamptonshire, c. 1520, glass and lead

UNDERSTANDING TUDOR ART

During the Tudor age artists had to follow accepted rules. They could only use certain materials and paint or sculpt traditional subjects. Changes did not happen as often or as quickly as they do today. Yet the achievements, inventions and discoveries made during Tudor times meant that changes and developments did occur in art, too. Religious changes forced artists to think of new ideas. Renaissance art that amazed the rest of Europe came late to England, bringing a style of its own when it did. New methods and equipment gave artists the chance to develop new skills.

Curious art

Wealthy people ordered colourful wall-hangings, panel paintings, or portraits for their homes to impress other people. Some people bought carpets from foreign lands, but not to put on the floors. Look again at Holbein's portrait of Georg Gisze on page 15. Rich people put their carpets on tables.

This curious picture has a curious name. It is called anamorphosis, a Greek word that means "transform". Close your right eye, and hold the right-hand side of the picture close to your left eye. Now you can see the face and background properly.

Prince Edward, 1546, William Scrotts, (worked from 1537–53) 42.5 x 160cm (17 x 63in), oil on panel

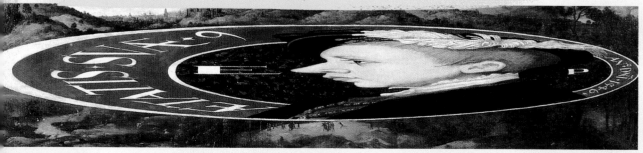

Mr. Symonds of Norfolk, *1595–1600, artist unknown, 76 x 96.5cm (30 x 38in), oil on panel*

Three years after Holbein died, William Scrotts became King's Painter to Henry VIII. He had picked up many ideas from Holbein and he knew all the latest fashions in court painting. As well as several portraits of Henry VIII's family, Scrotts painted the unusual picture of Prince Edward on page 28.

This is a fine example of how ordinary gentlemen began to commission portraits of themselves. We can see that Mr. Symonds was a gentleman because there is a hooded falcon on his hand. Only gentlemen went hawking. Also, he probably owned the ploughed fields behind him. But we know that the artist was not too expensive as he was not very skilled. The horse looks like a rocking horse with all its legs apart at once, and Mr. Symonds is too large for his horse. The most skilful artists charged a lot of money – probably more than Mr. Symonds could afford.

TIMELINE

1485	Henry Tudor is crowned Henry VII.
1497	Hans Holbein the Younger is born.
1500	Oil paints become popular.
1509	Henry VIII becomes king. First known wallpaper is produced.
1514	Building of Hampton Court Palace is started.
1516	Mary I is born.
1532	Hans Holbein moves to England and paints his portrait of Georg Gisze.
1533	Elizabeth I is born.
1536	Holbein paints a portrait of Henry VIII, and is made Court Painter.
1537	Edward VI is born.
1538	Henry VIII's palace of Nonsuch is started. Hengrave Hall is completed.
1543	Hans Holbein dies.
1546	William Scrotts paints portraits of Prince Edward.
1547	Edward VI becomes king. Nicholas Hilliard is born.
1553	Mary I becomes queen.
1558	Elizabeth I becomes queen.
1563	Foxe's *Book of Martyrs* is published.
1564	Michelangelo Buonarotti dies. William Shakespeare is born.
1565	The graphite pencil is invented in Switzerland.
1584	Nicholas Hilliard is made chief portraitist to Elizabeth I.
1588	The Spanish Armada tries to invade England, but is defeated.
1592	Marcus Geeraerts the Younger paints the "Ditchley" portrait of Elizabeth I.
1595	Walter Raleigh explores part of South America.
1603	Elizabeth I dies aged 70.

FIND OUT MORE

You can find out more about Tudor art in books and on the Internet. Use a search engine such as www.yahooligans.com to search for information. A search for the words "Tudor art" will bring back lots of results, but it may be difficult to find the information you want. Try refining your search to look for some of the people and ideas mentioned in this book, such as "Hans Holbein" or "miniature portraits".

More books to read

Adams, Simon. *Eyewitness Guides: Tudor*. London: Dorling Kindersley, 2004

Barber, Nicola. *History in Art: Tudor England*. Oxford: Raintree, 2005

GLOSSARY

alabaster translucent (slightly see-through) creamy-white stone

allegory picture of something that is being used to mean something else

apprentice young person who learns a trade or craft under the direction of a skilled worker

architecture design and construction of buildings

bronze brownish-gold metal, made of a mixture of copper and tin

buttress thick stone or brick pillar built against the outside of a wall to strengthen and support it

canvas strong woven cloth, traditionally made of hemp or linen

chisel metal tool with sharp edges used for carving

composition arrangement of a piece of art

easel stand used to support a painting

file metal tool with a rough surface to smooth the edges of carvings

fleur-de-lys stylised design of a lily with three petals joined together at the bottom

fresco wall painting made on damp, fresh plaster (fresco means "fresh" in Italian)

gargoyle stone spout to carry water off a roof, and often carved to look like a monster

gilt gold-like metal or a metal covered thinly with gold

guild society of craftsmen who all do the same job. They have to pay to join and must obey guild rules.

gum arabic glue-like gum

illuminated (manuscript) decorated handwritten book or document, usually in gold, silver, and brilliant colours

kiln extremely hot oven used to heat materials such as clay or pottery

marble hard rock that can be polished to a shine. It comes in all sorts of colours, some with swirly patterns.

martyr person who is killed for their religious beliefs

masque dance or play where the performers wear masks

mason someone who cuts, shapes, and builds in stone and brick

movable type first form of printing using metal letters, invented in Germany by Johann Gutenberg in 1455

pageant colourful parade of people

pastel soft, coloured chalk (from the Italian word pasta, meaning paste)

patrons people who buy artists' work

perspective way of showing space or distance on a flat surface

pigment coloured powder that gives paint its colour

portrait picture of a real person or animal

Renaissance the word means "rebirth" and describes the new interest in classical art and learning. The Renaissance lasted from about 1400 to about 1520.

stained glass pieces of coloured glass held in place by strips of lead to make a picture

succeed take a person's place after they have died

tempera pigment mixed with egg yolk, making a quick-drying paint

vellum fine parchment, like a smooth paper

Index

Numbers in plain type (24)
refer to the text.

Numbers in bold type (**28**)
refer to an illustration.